MF

David & Charles Cross Stitch Collection

A DAVID & CHARLES BOOK

First published in the UK in 2004

Designs copyright © Sue Cook,
Claire Crompton, Sam Hawkins,
Brenda Keyes, Helen Philipps 2004
Text, layout, photographs copyright
© David & Charles 2004

Distributed in North America
by F&W Publications, Inc.
4700 East Galbraith Road
Cincinnati, OH 45236
1-800-289-0963

Sue Cook, Claire Crompton, Sam
Hawkins, Brenda Keyes and Helen
Philipps have asserted their right to
be identified as authors of this work
in accordance with the Copyright,
Designs and Patents Act, 1988.

The publisher has endeavoured to
contact all contributors of text and
pictures for permission to reproduce.

A catalogue record for this book is
available from the British Library.

ISBN 0 7153 1755 5

Printed in Singapore by KHL
for David & Charles
Brunel House Newton Abbot Devon

Visit our website at
www.davidandcharles.co.uk

David & Charles books are
available from all good bookshops;
alternatively you can contact our
Orderline on (0) 1626 334555
or write to us at FREEPOST
EX2 110, David & Charles Direct,
Newton Abbot, TQ12 4ZZ (no
stamp required UK mainland).

Christmas Blessings

Contents

The Stitched Designs	2–3
MERRY CHRISTMAS AROUND THE WORLD	4–5
PEACE BE TO THIS HOUSE	6–7
A GAELIC BLESSING	8–9
CHRISTMAS TREAT AND TOPIARY CHRISTMAS	10
SANTA HEART AND CHRISTMAS WINDOW	11
WINTER'S TALE	12–13
Stitching Advice	14–16

Merry Christmas
Around the World
© Brenda Keyes

Christmas Treat
© Helen Philipps

Topiary Christmas
© Helen Philipps

Peace Be
To This House
© Sue Cook

2

A Gaelic Blessing
© Sue Cook

Santa Heart
© Sam Hawkins

Christmas Window
© Claire Crompton

Winter's Tale
© Helen Philipps

Noeliniz
kutlu
olsun

MERR
CHRISTM

Nadolig

e

Llawen

Glædelig
Jul

Nollaig faoi
shéan agus
faoi shonas
duit

VROLIJK
KERSTMIS

Fröhliche

Weihnachte

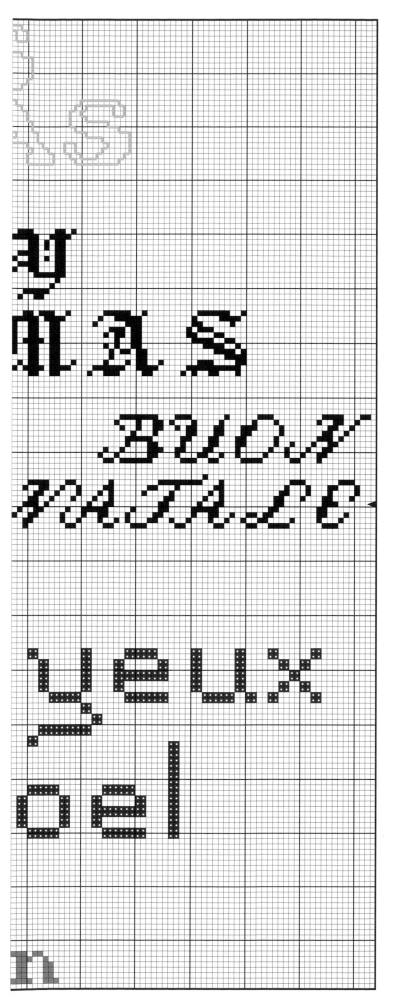

Merry Christmas Around the World

DMC PERLE COTTON NO. 5

Cross stitch

■	815
╱	935
■	518
⊡	321
▨	895
▨	936

Backstitch

━	115 variegated
━	909
━	935

Felices Pascuas	Spanish
Noeliniz kutlu olsun	Turkish
Nadolig Llawen	Welsh
Gledelig Jul	Norwegian
Buon Natale	Italian
Nollaig faoi shéan agus faoi shonas duit	Irish
Vrolijk Kerstmis	Dutch
Joyeaux Noel	French
Fröhliche Weihnachten	German

MERRY CHRISTMAS AROUND THE WORLD	
STITCH COUNT	200 x 177
DESIGN SIZE	36 x 40cm (14 x 16in)
FABRIC USED	Evenweave 25-count white Dublin linen, over 2 fabric threads
THREADS USED	See key: 1 strand perlé cotton No.5 for cross stitch and backstitch

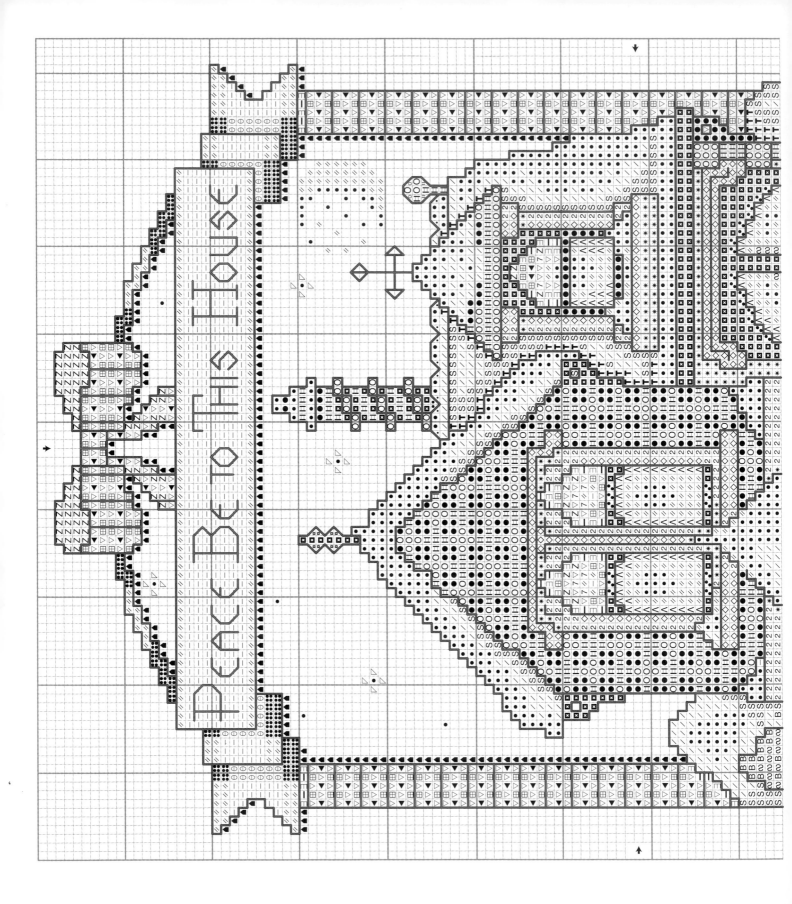

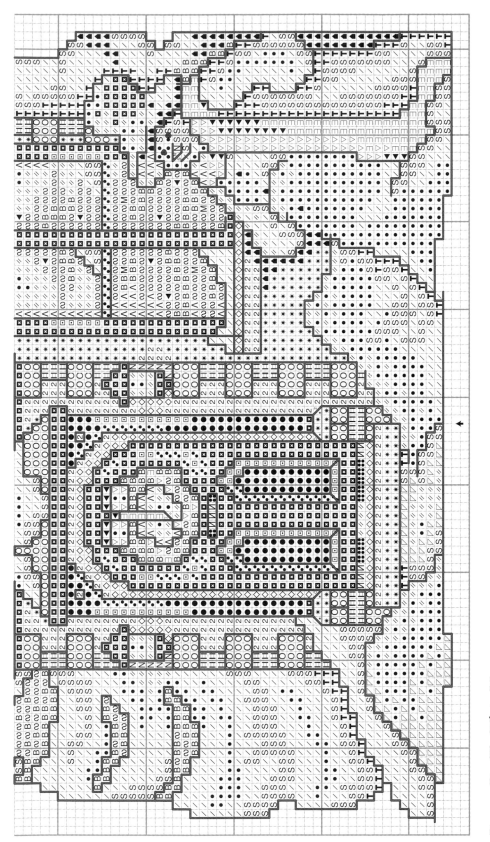

Peace Be To This House

Peace Be To This House	
STITCH COUNT	90 x 133
DESIGN SIZE	16.3 x 24cm (6½ x 9½in)
FABRIC USED	Evenweave 28-count royal blue, over 2 fabric threads
THREADS USED	See key: 2 strands of stranded cotton (floss) for cross stitch, 2 strands for blue backstitch, 1 strand for brown backstitch and 1 strand for French knots

DMC STRANDED COTTON
Cross stitch

··	01	white
▼▼	349	dark peach
▷▷	351	peach
••	434	light golden brown
▣▣	435	very light golden brown
MM	553	violet
⌐⌐	699	very dark Christmas green
ZZ	701	medium Christmas green
▦▦	703	very light Christmas green
77	704	ultra light Christmas green
——	712	cream
ΛΛ	725	topaz
◇◇	727	very light topaz

θθ	738	very light tan
ИИ	782	dark topaz
TT	798	dark Delft blue
SS	799	medium Delft blue
⁄⁄	800	light Delft blue
●●	801	dark coffee brown
ΞΞ	817	very dark coral red
◀◀	823	dark navy blue
HH	918	dark red copper
OO	921	copper
NN	922	light copper
22	3041	medium silver plum
◇◇	3042	light silver plum

BB	3345	very dark yellow green
⌐⌐	3347	medium yellow green
▣▣	3371	black brown
**	3740	dark silver plum
▽▽	3747	very light blue violet
▦▦	3820	dark straw

Backstitch

——	838	very dark beige brown
——	797	royal blue

French knots

●	823	dark navy blue

A GAELIC BLESSING

Deep peace of the running wave to you

Deep peace of the flowing air to you

Deep peace of the quiet earth to you

Deep peace of the watching shepherds to you

Deep peace of the Son of Peace to you

A Gaelic Blessing

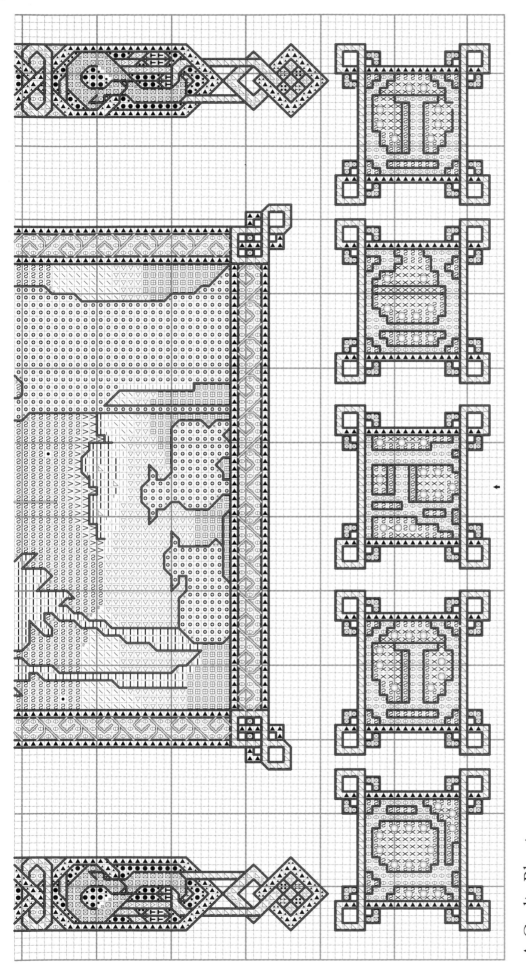

DMC STRANDED COTTON
Cross stitch

· ·	01	white
— —	336	navy blue
X X	340	medium violet blue
V V	341	light violet blue
M M	553	violet
↗↗	725	topaz
▽▽	780	very dark topaz
⊠⊠	782	dark topaz
▲	783	medium topaz
▽▽	794	light cornflower blue
⊙⊙	823	dark navy blue
▶▶	838	very dark beige brown
●●	991	dark aquamarine
9 9	993	light aquamarine
N N	3045	dark yellow beige
↑↑	3047	light yellow beige
⟋⟋	3746	dark blue violet
⟋⟋	3747	very light blue violet
⊞⊞	3807	cornflower blue
T T	3814	aquamarine
– –	3823	ultra pale yellow
θ θ	3830	terracotta

Backstitch

——		Kreinik fine braid (no. 8) 221 antique gold
—	823	dark navy blue
—	838	very dark beige brown

French knots

●	838	very dark beige brown

Beads

○		DMC seed beads V2.0820 antique gold

A GAELIC BLESSING	
STITCH COUNT	124 x 161
DESIGN SIZE	21.7 x 29.2cm (8½ x 11½in)
FABRIC USED	Evenweave 28-count natural linen, over 2 fabric threads
THREADS USED	See key: 2 strands of stranded cotton (floss) for cross stitch and 1 strand for backstitch
EMBELLISHMENTS	Seed beads: antique gold, over lettering

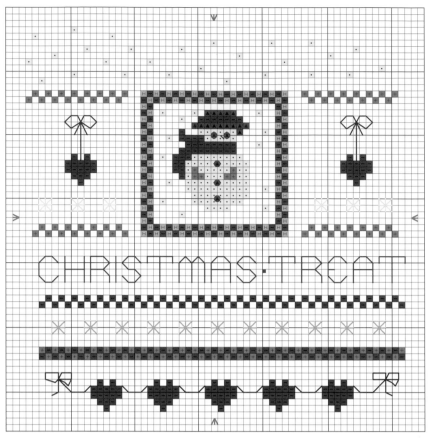
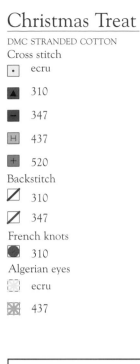

Christmas Treat

DMC STRANDED COTTON

Cross stitch

- · ecru
- ▲ 310
- ━ 347
- H 437
- ✚ 520

Backstitch

- ╱ 310
- ╱ 347

French knots

- ● 310

Algerian eyes

- ▦ ecru
- ✳ 437

CHRISTMAS TREAT	
STITCH COUNT	59 x 60
DESIGN SIZE	9.5 x 9.5cm (3¾ x 3¾in)
FABRIC USED	Evenweave 32-count natural linen, over 2 fabric threads
THREADS USED	See key: 2 strands of stranded cotton (floss) for cross stitch, French knots and Algerian eyes and 1 strand for backstitch
EMBELLISHMENTS (OPTIONAL)	Button: snowman (or stitch motif instead)

Topiary Christmas

DMC STRANDED COTTON

Cross stitch

- S ecru
- ✚ 501
- ↑ 504
- U 3721

Backstitch

- ╱ 500

TOPIARY CHRISTMAS	
STITCH COUNT	37 x 45
DESIGN SIZE	6.7 x 8.3cm (2⅝ x 3¼in)
FABRIC USED	Evenweave 28-count natural linen, over 2 fabric threads
THREADS USED	See key: 2 strands of stranded cotton (floss) for cross stitch and 1 for backstitch
EMBELLISHMENTS	Charm: silver star (at position of black dot)

Santa Heart

DMC STRANDED COTTON

Cross stitch		Backstitch	
·	blanc	⟋	310
■	310	⟋	321
–	321	⟋	413
S	700	⟋	632
+	758		
→	762		
=	776		
U	948		
✕	3705		
↑	3773		
％	3774		

SANTA HEART	
STITCH COUNT	48 x 38
DESIGN SIZE	9 x 7cm (3½ x 2¾in)
FABRIC USED	Aida 14-count white, over 1 block
THREADS USED	See key: 2 strands of stranded cotton (floss) for cross stitch and backstitch
EMBELLISHMENTS	Buttons: 2 wooden heart-shaped, sewn on either side of design

Christmas Window

DMC STRANDED COTTON

Cross stitch		Backstitch	
✓	168	⟋	gold
✕	309		
Z	498		
⊞	550		
N	797		
<	799		
⑤	820		
∧	844		
⊙	986		
C	988		
U	3837		
·	3865		
4	gold		

CHRISTMAS WINDOW	
STITCH COUNT	39 x 61
DESIGN SIZE	7 x 11cm (2¾ x 4⅜in)
FABRIC USED	Aida 14-count white, over 1 block
THREADS USED	See key: 2 strands of stranded cotton (floss) for cross stitch and 1 strand for backstitch

Winter's Tale

DMC STRANDED COTTON

Cross stitch		Backstitch	
·	ecru	☐	ecru
N	301	⊘	301
+	310	⊘	310
→	317	⊘	317
↑	340	⊘	340
U	347	⊘	500
I	437	⊘	501
▽	445	⊘	730
Z	500	⊘	816
‖	501	⊘	930
H	730		
←	742	Madeira Glamour	
T	816	⊘	2442 light silver
4	930		
∩	3023	French knots	
▢	3362	☐	ecru
⅂	3721	●	310
=	3746	●	347
T	3826	●	501
S	3827	●	742

Madeira Glamour

O	2442 light silver

BACKSTITCH DETAILS	
317	Lettering 'The mistletoe hung in the castle hall. . .'
500	All pine needle sprigs, beside cottage door and lettering 'There seems a magic. . .'
501	Sheep picture box outline and mistletoe stem below cottage
730	Mistletoe stems beside robin
930	Stocking outline and lettering for 'Mistletoe Cottage'

WINTER'S TALE	
STITCH COUNT	194 x 150
DESIGN SIZE	35 x 26.6cm (13¾ x 10½in)
FABRIC USED	Evenweave 28-count grey, over 2 fabric threads
THREADS USED	See key: 2 strands of stranded cotton (floss) for cross stitch, French knots and Algerian eyes (the silver stars) and 1 strand for backstitch and lettering
EMBELLISHMENTS (OPTIONAL)	Buttons: 2 lanterns, 1 gingerbread man, 1 star (or stitch motifs instead)

Stitching Advice

The following section is relevant throughout the David & Charles *Cross Stitch Collection* series, not just the charts in this book. It will provide you with all the information you need to stitch the designs charted.

MATERIALS

FABRICS

Fabrics used for counted cross stitch are woven so they have the same number of threads or blocks to 2.5cm (1in), both horizontally and vertically. The two main fabric types used are blockweaves such as Aida, and even-weaves such as linen. Cross stitch can also be worked on other fabrics such as waste canvas, plastic canvas and stitching (perforated) paper.

AIDAS These fabrics are woven in blocks and are available in many colours and counts – 8, 11, 14, 16, 18 and 20 blocks to 2.5cm (1in). They are made from various fibres and as different width bands. When stitching on Aida, one block on the fabric corresponds to one square on a chart and each cross stitch is worked over one block.

EVENWEAVES These fabrics are woven singly and are made from various fibres and as different width bands. They are also available in many different colours and counts. When stitching on evenweave, each cross stitch is usually worked over two threads of the fabric.

WASTE CANVAS This is designed for stitching on fabrics where cross stitching wouldn't normally be possible because the threads are uneven, such as clothing. To use, tack (baste) a piece of waste canvas large enough for the design into position on to the chosen article and cross stitch the design through both fabrics. When all stitching is complete, dampen the canvas and use tweezers to draw out the threads. You may find it easier to work backstitches after the canvas has been removed.

PLASTIC CANVAS This is a rigid but flexible mesh-like material that can be cut and assembled into three-dimensional objects. It is available in various counts and as pre-cut shapes. Cross stitches are worked over intersections of the mesh.

STITCHING PAPER Cross stitch designs can be worked on perforated paper which can then be cut, folded and glued to make a variety of items such as cards, bookmarks and notebook covers. The right side is the smoother side of the paper and cross stitch is normally worked with three strands of stranded cotton (floss) and backstitch with two.

THREADS

The most commonly used thread for counted embroidery is stranded cotton (floss) but there are many other types available, including rayons, space-dyed or variegated threads, perlé cottons and metallic threads.

STRANDED COTTON (FLOSS) This six-stranded thread can be bought by the skein in hundreds of colours with ranges made by DMC, Anchor and Madeira (see DMC/Anchor conversion chart at the front of this book). Colours can be mixed or 'tweeded' in the needle. The stitching information with the charts will tell you how many strands to use for a design.

VARIEGATED THREADS There are many lovely variegated threads available now. The chart keys give the name and code of the thread used. When stitching with variegated threads work cross stitches as complete stitches, not in two journeys or the colour sequence will be spoiled.

METALLICS AND BLENDING FILAMENTS Metallic threads are available in many gorgeous colours and finishes from various companies and they can be used in cross stitch designs to create glitter and interest. Blending filaments can be stitched with stranded cotton (floss) to create an over-all sparkle to a design. Use shorter lengths of thread when working with metallics to avoid tangles and excessive wear on the thread.

TAPESTRY WOOL (YARN) Many cross stitch designs can be stitched on canvas in tapestry wool (yarn) instead of stranded cotton (floss), using half cross stitch or tent stitch instead of cross stitch. Ask at needlework shops for suppliers and colour conversions from stranded cotton (floss).

EQUIPMENT

Very little equipment is needed for cross stitch embroidery and the following basics are all you need to get you started.

NEEDLES Use blunt tapestry needles for counted cross stitch. The commonest sizes used are 24 and 26 but the size depends on your project and personal preference. Avoid leaving a needle in the fabric unless it is gold plated or it may cause marks. A beading needle (or fine 'sharp' needle), which is much thinner, will be needed to attach beads.

SCISSORS Use dressmaker's shears for cutting fabric and a small, sharp pair of pointed scissors for cutting embroidery threads.

FRAMES AND HOOPS These are not essential but if you use one, choose one large enough to hold the complete design, to avoid marking the fabric and flattening stitches.

TECHNIQUES

USING CHARTS

The designs in this series are worked from black and white charts with symbols, or colour charts with a black and/or white symbol to aid colour identification. Each square, both occupied and unoccupied, represents one block of Aida or two threads of linen, unless stated otherwise. Each occupied square equals one cross stitch. Some charts also have three-quarter cross stitches (sometimes called fractional stitches) and these usually occupy part of a square, either a triangle or a small square. French knots are indicated by circles, usually coloured in the colour charts and labelled in the key or on the chart. Backstitch (and some-times long stitch) is shown on charts by straight lines, usually coloured in the colour charts, with the code either on the chart or in the key. Arrows at the sides of the charts allow you to find the centre easily.

CALCULATING DESIGN SIZE

Each project gives the stitch count and finished design size but if you plan to work the design on a different count you will need to be able to calculate the finished size. To do this, count the number of stitches in the design and divide this by the fabric count number, e.g., 140 stitches x 140 stitches ÷ by 14-count = a design size of 10 x 10in (25.4 x 25.4cm). Remember that working on evenweave usually means working over two threads not one, so divide the fabric count by 2 before you start. See the bottom of page 15 for a quick stitch count table.

PREPARING FABRICS

The sizes given with the charts are for the finished design size only, therefore you will need to add about 10–12.5cm (4–5in) to both measurements when cutting embroidery fabric, to allow enough fabric around the edges for working and for making up later.

Before you begin stitching, press your embroidery fabric if necessary and trim the selvage or any rough edges. Work from the middle of the fabric and middle of the chart where possible to ensure your design is centred on the fabric. Find the middle of the fabric by folding it in four and pressing lightly. Mark the folds with tailor's chalk or with lines of tacking (basting) following a fabric thread. When working with linen, prepare as described above but also sew a narrow hem around all raw edges to preserve them for finishing later.

STARTING AND FINISHING STITCHING

Unless indicated otherwise, begin stitching in the middle of a design to ensure an adequate margin for making up. Start and finish stitching neatly, avoiding knots which create a lumps.

KNOTLESS LOOP START This start can be used with an even number of strands i.e., 2, 4 or 6. To stitch with two strands, begin with one strand about 80cm (30in). Double the thread and thread the needle with the two ends. Put the needle up through the fabric from the wrong side, where you intend to begin stitching, leaving the loop at the back (see diagram top of page 15). Form a half cross stitch, put the needle back through the fabric and through the waiting loop to anchor the stitch.

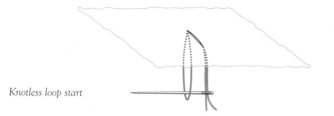

Knotless loop start

AWAY WASTE KNOT START Start this way if using an odd number of strands. Thread the needle with the number of strands required and knot the end. Insert the needle into the right side of the fabric, away from where you wish to begin stitching (see diagram below). Stitch towards the knot and cut it off when the threads are anchored. Alternatively, snip off the knot, thread a needle and work under a few stitches to anchor.

Away waste knot start

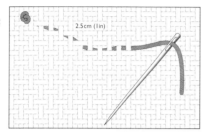

2.5cm (1in)

FINISHING STITCHING At the back of the work, pass the needle and thread under several stitches and snip off the loose end close to the stitching. Begin new colours by passing through stitches on the back in a similar way.

NUMBER OF STRANDS

Stranded cotton (floss) is available in six-stranded skeins and different numbers of strands will be needed for use on different gauges of fabric. Generally two strands are used for cross stitch and one for backstitch but the following table gives further advice.

HOW MANY STRANDS?

FABRIC	NUMBER OF STRANDS OF STRANDED COTTON
6-count Aida	6 or 8 for cross stitch, 2 for backstitch
8-count Aida	6 for cross stitch, 2 for backstitch
11-count Aida & 22-count evenweave (over 2 threads)	3 for cross stitch, 1 for backstitch
14-count Aida & 28-count evenweave (over 2 threads)	2 or 3 for cross stitch, 1 for backstitch
16-count Aida & 32-count evenweave (over 2 threads)	2 for cross stitch, 1 for backstitch
18-count Aida & 36-count evenweave (over 2 threads)	1 or 2 for cross stitch, 1 for backstitch

BLENDING THREADS

Many threads can be used together in the needle to create new colour combinations or to add the shine and glitter of metallic threads such as blending filament. Simply thread the needle with both threads, usually one strand of each, and stitch as normal.

CHANGING NAMES AND DATES

Some cross stitch designs feature names and dates or other wording which you will need to alter using the alphabet provided (or one of your own favourites). Before you begin to stitch, ensure the words will fit the space by counting the squares in the space available (width and height) and marking this on square graph paper. Pencil the letters or numbers on the graph paper, remembering the spaces between letters and words.

ATTACHING BEADS, CHARMS AND BUTTONS

Bead positions are shown on the charts as circles (coloured in the colour charts), with details of the bead type in the key. You might find using a frame or hoop is helpful to keep the fabric taut as you pull the thread firmly to keep the beads in position. Attach beads using a beading needle or very fine 'sharp' needle, thread which matches the bead colour and a half cross stitch (or a full cross stitch if you prefer).

Charm and button positions are usually shown on the chart or described in the key or shown on the photograph of the model. Attach charms and buttons with matching thread.

If you cannot find the beads, charms or buttons suggested on the charts simply substitute something else – there is a wealth to choose from nowadays.

USING RIBBON

Narrow ribbon can be used to create additional interest in a cross stitch design. It may be used to form stitches, such as simple straight stitches, lazy daisy stitch or detached chain stitch. It can also be couched flat on to the fabric and held in place with cross stitches or narrow straight stitches or beads. Ribbon can also be threaded through evenweave fabric after several threads have been removed to create a channel.

TIPS FOR PERFECT STITCHING

● Organize your threads before you start a project as this will help to avoid confusion later. Always include the manufacturer's name and the shade number.

● Separate the strands on a skein of stranded cotton (floss) before taking the number you need to stitch with. Realign them before threading your needle.

● If using a frame, try to avoid a hoop as it will stretch the fabric and leave a mark that may be difficult to remove.

● Plan your route around a chart, counting over short distances wherever possible to avoid mistakes.

● Work your cross stitch in two directions in a sewing movement – half cross stitch in one direction and then cover those original stitches with the second row. This forms single vertical lines on the back that are very neat and give somewhere to finish raw ends. For neat work the top stitches should all face the same direction.

● If adding a backstitch outline, always add it after the cross stitch has been completed to prevent the solid line being broken.

QUICK STITCH COUNTS (see Calculating Design Size, page 14)

FABRIC	STITCH COUNT									
	20	30	40	50	60	70	80	90	100	110
11-count Aida & 22-count evenweave	1¾in (4.6cm)	2¾in (7cm)	3½in (9.2cm)	4½in (11.5cm)	5½in (13.8cm)	6¼in (16cm)	7¼in (18.5cm)	8⅛in (20.7cm)	9in (23cm)	10in (25.4cm)
14-count Aida & 28-count evenweave	1½in (3.6cm)	2⅛in (5.4cm)	2¾in (7.2cm)	3½in (9cm)	4¼in (10.8cm)	5in (12.7cm)	5¾in (14.5cm)	6½in (16.3cm)	7⅛in (18cm)	7⅞in (20cm)
16-count Aida & 32-count evenweave	1¼in (3cm)	1⅞in (4.8cm)	2½in (6.3cm)	3⅛in (8cm)	3¾in (9.5cm)	4¼in (11cm)	5in (12.7cm)	5½in (14.3cm)	6¼in (16cm)	6¾in (17.4cm)
18-count Aida & 36-count evenweave	1⅛in (2.8cm)	1½in (4.2cm)	2¼in (5.6cm)	2¾in (7cm)	3⅜in (8.5cm)	3¾in (9.8cm)	4½in (11.3cm)	5in (12.7cm)	5½in (14cm)	6⅛in (15.5cm)

THE STITCHES

ALGERIAN EYE

This star-shaped stitch is a pulled stitch which creates 'holes' in the fabric. It can be worked over two or four threads of evenweave and is more successful on evenweave than Aida.

Start to the left of a vertical thread and work from left to right around each stitch in an anticlockwise direction (or vice versa but keeping each stitch the same). Pass the needle down through the central hole and pull quite firmly so a small hole is formed in the centre. Take care that trailing threads do not cover the hole as you progress.

 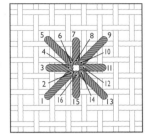

BACKSTITCH

Backstitch is used for outlining, to add detail or emphasis and for lettering. It is added after the cross stitch to prevent the backstitch line being broken. It is usually indicated on a chart by solid lines with the suggested shade on the chart or key.

Follow the numbered sequence, right, working the stitches over one block of Aida or two threads of evenweave.

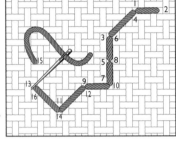

CROSS STITCH

This simple little stitch is the most commonly used stitch in this book. Cross stitches can be worked singly or in two journeys but for neat stitching, keep the top stitch facing the same direction. It does not matter which way it faces but it should be the same for the whole project.

CROSS STITCH ON AIDA

Cross stitch on Aida fabric is normally worked over one block.

To work one complete cross stitch
Follow the numbered sequence in the diagram: bring the needle up through the fabric at the bottom left corner, cross one block of the fabric and insert the needle at the top right corner. Push the needle

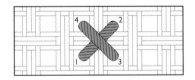

through and bring it up at the bottom right corner, ready to complete the stitch in the top left corner. To work the adjacent stitch, bring the needle up at the bottom right-hand corner of the first stitch.

To work cross stitches in two journeys
Work the first leg of the cross stitch as above but instead of completing the stitch, work the adjacent half stitch and continue on to the end of the row. Complete all the crosses by working the other diagonals on the return journey.

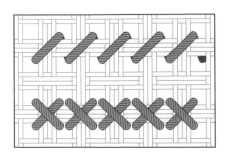

CROSS STITCH ON EVENWEAVE

Cross stitch on evenweave is usually worked over two threads of the fabric in each direction to even out any oddities in the thickness of the fibres. Bring the needle up to the left of a vertical thread, which will make it easier to spot counting mistakes. Work your cross stitch in two directions, as described before. This forms neat, single vertical lines on the back and gives somewhere to finish raw ends.

THREE-QUARTER CROSS STITCH

Three-quarter cross stitch is a fractional stitch which produces the illusion of curves when working cross stitch designs. The stitch can be formed on either Aida or evenweave but is more successful on evenweave. They are usually shown on charts as a triangle (half square).

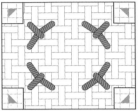

Work the first half of a cross stitch as usual. Work the second 'quarter' stitch over the top and down into the central hole to anchor the first half of the stitch. If using Aida, you will need to push the needle through the centre of a block of the fabric. Where two three-quarter stitches lie back-to-back in the space of one full cross stitch, work both of the respective 'quarter' stitches into the central hole.

Some designs use half cross stitch and quarter cross stitch and these are, respectively, a single diagonal line and a quarter of a diagonal line.

FRENCH KNOT

French knots are shown on charts as circles, coloured on colour charts. Bring the needle through to the front of the fabric and wind the thread around the needle twice. Put the needle partly through to the back, one thread or part of a block away from the entry point, to stop the stitch being pulled to the wrong side. Gently pull the thread you have wound so that it sits snugly at the point where the needle enters the fabric. Pull the needle through to the back and you should have a perfect knot in position. For bigger knots, add more thread to the needle.

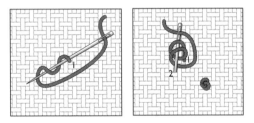

LONG STITCH

This is a long, straight stitch used to create animals' whiskers and so on. Bring the needle and thread up where the stitch is to start and down where the chart indicates it should finish. Occasionally long stitches are couched down – that is, held in place along their length with little stitches, as shown here.

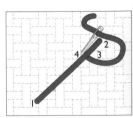

TENT STITCH

This stitch is usually used for working with wool (yarn) on canvas. It looks like half cross stitch from the front but has long, slanting stitches on the back, which

means it uses more yarn and thus is harder wearing. Follow the diagram, taking the needle under the stitches from right to left.